Meniere's Disease

Kishan Kumawat

ISBN 978-93-5667-765-4

Published in India 2023 by Pencil

A brand of
One Point Six Technologies Pvt. Ltd.
Unit no. 26, Ground Floor, Building A1,
Wadala Truck Terminal Road,
Near Post Office, Antop Hill, Mumbai - 400037
E connect@thepencilapp.com
W www.thepencilapp.com

Author biography

Kishan Kumawat is a talented author from Rajasthan, India, with many years of experience in writing. His passion for helping others has led him to specialise in self-help books, and his latest work focuses on providing support and guidance for those living with illness. Kishan's unique insights and knowledge on the topic make him a valuable resource for anyone looking to better understand and manage challenging illnesses. Kishan's work has already helped many people around the world, and his dedication to his craft promises even more great things to come.

CONTENTS

Understanding Meniere's Disease

Meniere's disease is a disorder of the inner ear that causes vertigo, hearing loss, tinnitus, and a feeling of fullness or pressure in the affected ear. Named after the French physician Prosper Meniere, who first described the condition in 1861, Meniere's disease is a chronic and often unpredictable condition that can significantly impact a person's quality of life.

Understanding the underlying causes of Meniere's disease remains a topic of ongoing research, and several theories have been proposed. One leading theory suggests that Meniere's disease is caused by a buildup of fluid in the inner ear, leading to increased pressure and damage to the delicate sensory cells responsible for balance and hearing. This fluid buildup is thought to result from a malfunction of the body's fluid regulation system, although the exact mechanisms involved are not yet fully understood.

Another possible contributing factor to Meniere's disease is a problem with blood flow to the inner ear. Some studies suggest that people with Meniere's disease may have reduced blood flow to the inner ear, leading to damage and dysfunction of the sensory cells.

In addition to these physical causes, psychological and emotional factors may also play a role in Meniere's disease. Stress, anxiety, and depression are common among people with Meniere's disease, and some studies have suggested that these conditions may contribute to the onset or severity of Meniere's symptoms.

The hallmark symptom of Meniere's disease is vertigo, which is characterized by a spinning sensation or a feeling of being off-balance. Vertigo episodes can last anywhere from a few minutes to several hours and may be accompanied by nausea, vomiting, sweating, and anxiety. Some people with Meniere's disease experience vertigo attacks only occasionally, while others may have several attacks per week.

Hearing loss is another common symptom of Meniere's disease, and it typically affects one ear more than the other. The hearing loss may be temporary or permanent and may fluctuate over time. Tinnitus, or ringing in the ear, is also a common symptom of Meniere's disease and can be persistent or intermittent.

Diagnosing Meniere's disease can be challenging, as there is no specific test that can definitively confirm the condition. Instead, doctors typically rely on a combination of symptoms, medical history, and hearing and balance tests to make a diagnosis. Imaging tests such as an MRI may be ordered to rule out other potential causes of symptoms, such as a brain tumor or multiple sclerosis.

Treatment for Meniere's disease typically focuses on managing symptoms and preventing complications. Medications such as diuretics, antihistamines, and anti-nausea drugs may be prescribed to help manage vertigo and other symptoms. In some cases, injections of corticosteroids may be given directly into the inner ear to reduce inflammation and swelling.

In more severe cases of Meniere's disease, surgery may be recommended. Surgical options include procedures to remove excess fluid from the inner ear, to destroy the sensory cells responsible for vertigo, or to implant a device that helps regulate inner ear fluid levels.

Natural and alternative remedies such as acupuncture, dietary supplements, and herbal remedies may also be used to manage symptoms of Meniere's disease, although the efficacy of these treatments is not well established.

Living with Meniere's disease can be challenging, but there are several strategies that can help individuals cope with the condition. Maintaining a healthy lifestyle, including regular exercise and a balanced diet, can help manage symptoms and improve overall health. Managing stress and anxiety through techniques such as meditation and relaxation exercises can also be helpful. It is important to communicate with friends, family, and healthcare providers about the impact of Meniere's disease on daily life and to seek support when needed.

Symptoms

Meniere's disease is a chronic condition of the inner ear that can cause a range of symptoms, including vertigo, hearing loss, tinnitus, and a feeling of fullness or pressure in the affected ear. These symptoms can be unpredictable and vary in severity from person to person, making Meniere's disease a challenging condition to manage.

Vertigo is one of the most common and disabling symptoms of Meniere's disease. Vertigo is a sensation of spinning or a feeling of being off-balance, and it can be triggered by sudden movements or changes in position. Vertigo episodes can last anywhere from a few minutes to several hours and may be accompanied by other symptoms such as nausea, vomiting, sweating, and anxiety. Some people with Meniere's disease may experience vertigo only occasionally, while others may have several episodes per week.

Hearing loss is another common symptom of Meniere's disease and typically affects one ear more than the other. The hearing loss may be temporary or permanent and may fluctuate over time. People with Meniere's disease may also experience a sensation of pressure or fullness in the affected ear, which can be uncomfortable and distracting.

Tinnitus, or ringing in the ear, is another common symptom of Meniere's disease. The sound can be high-pitched or low-pitched and may be continuous or intermittent. Tinnitus can be persistent and may interfere with sleep and concentration.

In addition to these primary symptoms, people with Meniere's disease may experience a range of secondary symptoms that can impact their quality of life. Fatigue, dizziness, and balance problems are common among people with Meniere's disease, and these symptoms can make it difficult to perform everyday tasks such as driving or working.

Managing Meniere's disease symptoms can be challenging, but there are several strategies that can be helpful. Medications such as diuretics, antihistamines, and anti-nausea drugs may be prescribed to manage vertigo and other symptoms. In some cases, injections of corticosteroids may be given directly into the inner ear to reduce inflammation and swelling.

Surgery may be recommended in more severe cases of Meniere's disease. Surgical options include procedures to remove excess fluid from the inner ear, to destroy the sensory cells responsible for vertigo, or to implant a device that helps regulate inner ear fluid levels.

Natural and alternative remedies such as acupuncture, dietary supplements, and herbal remedies may also be used to manage symptoms of Meniere's disease, although the efficacy of these treatments is not well established.

In addition to medical treatments, there are several lifestyle changes that can help manage Meniere's disease symptoms. Eating a healthy diet and avoiding foods that can trigger symptoms such as caffeine, alcohol, and salt can be helpful. Regular exercise and stress management techniques such as meditation and relaxation exercises can also be beneficial.

Living with Meniere's disease can be challenging, but there are several resources available to help individuals manage their symptoms and improve their quality of life. Support groups, online forums, and educational resources can provide information and support to people with Meniere's disease and their families.

In conclusion, Meniere's disease is a chronic condition of the inner ear that can cause a range of symptoms including vertigo, hearing loss, tinnitus, and a feeling of fullness or pressure in the affected ear. These symptoms can be unpredictable and vary in severity from person to person, making Meniere's disease a challenging condition to manage. However, there are several strategies and treatments available that can help manage symptoms and improve quality of life. It is important for individuals with Meniere's disease to work closely with their healthcare providers and to seek support when needed.

Causes and Risk Factors

The exact causes of Meniere's disease are not well understood, but researchers believe that a combination of genetic and environmental factors may contribute to the development of the condition.

One possible cause of Meniere's disease is a buildup of fluid in the inner ear. The inner ear contains a system of canals and sacs filled with fluid that help regulate balance and hearing. If the fluid in these structures becomes imbalanced or if there is a blockage in the canals, it can cause symptoms such as vertigo, hearing loss, and tinnitus.

Another possible cause of Meniere's disease is damage to the inner ear due to injury or infection. The inner ear contains delicate structures such as hair cells and nerves that can be damaged by loud noises, infections, or other factors. Over time, this damage can lead to symptoms of Meniere's disease.

There may also be a genetic component to Meniere's disease, as some studies have suggested that certain gene mutations may increase the risk of developing the condition. However, more research is needed to fully understand the genetic factors involved in Meniere's disease.

Certain risk factors may increase the likelihood of developing Meniere's disease. Age is a significant risk factor, as Meniere's disease typically affects people between the ages of 40 and 60. Women are also more likely than men to develop Meniere's disease.

Other risk factors for Meniere's disease include a history of migraines, autoimmune disorders, and allergies. People who have a history of ear infections or have had head trauma may also be at increased risk for developing Meniere's disease.

Exposure to certain environmental factors may also increase the risk of Meniere's disease. Exposure to loud noises or certain chemicals such as solvents and heavy metals may increase the risk of developing inner ear damage and subsequent symptoms of Meniere's disease.

Diagnosis of Meniere's disease typically involves a combination of medical history, physical exam, and diagnostic tests such as hearing tests and imaging studies. Treatment options for Meniere's disease depend on the severity and frequency of symptoms, and may include medications, dietary changes, and in some cases, surgery.

In conclusion, the causes of Meniere's disease are not fully understood, but researchers believe that a combination of genetic and environmental factors may contribute to the development of the condition. Possible causes include a buildup of fluid in the inner ear, damage to the inner ear due to injury or infection, and genetic factors. Certain risk factors such as age, gender, and exposure to environmental factors may also increase the likelihood of developing Meniere's disease. If you experience symptoms of Meniere's disease, it is important to seek medical attention to receive an accurate diagnosis and appropriate treatment.

Medications

Medications can be an important part of the treatment plan for Meniere's disease, as they can help to alleviate symptoms such as vertigo, tinnitus, and hearing loss. However, not all medications are equally effective for all people with Meniere's disease, and it is important to work closely with a healthcare provider to determine the most appropriate treatment approach.

One class of medications commonly used to treat Meniere's disease is diuretics. Diuretics help to reduce the amount of fluid in the body, which can help to alleviate the buildup of fluid in the inner ear that can cause symptoms of Meniere's disease. Examples of diuretics commonly used for Meniere's disease include hydrochlorothiazide and spironolactone.

Another class of medications commonly used to treat Meniere's disease is vestibular suppressants. These medications work to suppress the signals from the inner ear that contribute to vertigo and other balance problems. Examples of vestibular suppressants commonly used for Meniere's disease include meclizine, diazepam, and lorazepam.

In some cases, corticosteroids may be used to treat Meniere's disease. Corticosteroids help to reduce inflammation in the inner ear, which can help to alleviate symptoms such as hearing loss and vertigo. Corticosteroids may be given orally or through injections into the ear.

Some people with Meniere's disease may also benefit from the use of anti-nausea medications. These medications can help to alleviate nausea and vomiting that can occur during episodes of vertigo.

In addition to medication, certain lifestyle changes may also be helpful for managing symptoms of Meniere's disease. For example, reducing salt intake can help to reduce fluid retention in the body, which can in turn reduce the buildup of fluid in the inner ear. Some people with Meniere's disease may also benefit from a low-sugar diet, as high blood sugar levels have been linked to an increased risk of vertigo.

In conclusion, medications can be an important part of the treatment plan for Meniere's disease, but it is important to work closely with a healthcare provider to determine the most appropriate medication and dosage for your specific needs. Diuretics, vestibular suppressants, corticosteroids, and anti-nausea medications are all commonly used to treat Meniere's disease. In addition to medication, certain lifestyle changes such as reducing salt intake and following a low-sugar diet may also be helpful for managing symptoms.

Surgery

Surgery is typically considered a last resort for treating Meniere's disease, as most people are able to manage their symptoms with medication and lifestyle changes. However, in some cases, surgery may be necessary if other treatments have been unsuccessful in managing symptoms or if symptoms are severe and significantly impacting quality of life.

One type of surgery commonly used for Meniere's disease is endolymphatic sac decompression. This surgery involves removing a portion of the bone that surrounds the endolymphatic sac, which is the part of the inner ear that helps to regulate fluid levels. By removing a portion of the bone, pressure on the endolymphatic sac is relieved, which can help to reduce symptoms of Meniere's disease. Endolymphatic sac decompression is typically performed on one ear at a time and can be done through a small incision behind the ear.

Another type of surgery that may be used for Meniere's disease is vestibular nerve section. This surgery involves cutting the vestibular nerve, which is the nerve that sends signals from the inner ear to the brain to help control balance. By cutting the vestibular nerve, the signals that contribute to vertigo and other balance problems are disrupted, which can help to alleviate symptoms of Meniere's disease. Vestibular nerve section is typically only performed on one ear and is done under general anesthesia.

In some cases, a more invasive surgery called labyrinthectomy may be necessary. This surgery involves removing a portion of the inner ear, which permanently disrupts the signals that contribute to vertigo and other balance problems. While labyrinthectomy can be highly effective in reducing symptoms of Meniere's disease, it also comes with significant risks, including complete hearing loss in the affected ear.

It is important to note that surgery is not always effective for treating Meniere's disease, and it is not without risks. In addition, not all people with Meniere's disease are good candidates for surgery. A healthcare provider will carefully evaluate a person's individual situation and make a recommendation based on the severity of their symptoms, overall health, and other factors.

In conclusion, while surgery is not the first line of treatment for Meniere's disease, it may be necessary in some cases if other treatments have been unsuccessful or if symptoms are severe and significantly impacting quality of life. Endolymphatic sac decompression, vestibular nerve section, and labyrinthectomy are all surgical options for Meniere's disease, but they come with risks and are not always effective for all people. It is important to work closely with a healthcare provider to determine the most appropriate treatment plan for your specific needs.

Natural and Alternative Remedies

While medication and lifestyle changes can be effective in managing symptoms of Meniere's disease, some people may also benefit from natural and alternative remedies. It is important to note that while these remedies may be helpful, they should not be used as a replacement for medical treatment. Always speak with a healthcare provider before starting any new treatments.

Here are some natural and alternative remedies that may help manage symptoms of Meniere's disease:

Acupuncture: Acupuncture is a form of traditional Chinese medicine that involves inserting thin needles into specific points on the body. Some people with Meniere's disease report that acupuncture has helped to reduce their symptoms.

Ginger: Ginger is a natural anti-inflammatory and may help to reduce inflammation in the inner ear, which can contribute to symptoms of Meniere's disease. It can be consumed in various forms, such as tea or supplements.

Ginkgo biloba: Ginkgo biloba is a natural supplement that is believed to improve blood flow to the brain, which may help to reduce symptoms of Meniere's disease.

Vitamin supplements: Certain vitamins, such as vitamin B6 and magnesium, may help to reduce symptoms of Meniere's disease. However, it is important to speak with a healthcare provider before taking any new supplements.

Yoga and meditation: Yoga and meditation may help to reduce stress and anxiety, which can exacerbate symptoms of Meniere's disease. Some people with Meniere's disease report that regular yoga and meditation practices have helped to reduce their symptoms.

Essential oils: Certain essential oils, such as peppermint and lavender, may help to reduce symptoms of Meniere's disease when used in aromatherapy. However, it is important to use essential oils safely and speak with a healthcare provider before use.

Chiropractic care: Chiropractic care may help to improve the function of the vestibular system, which can contribute to symptoms of Meniere's disease. However, it is important to work with a qualified chiropractor and speak with a healthcare provider before starting chiropractic treatment.

While these natural and alternative remedies may be helpful in managing symptoms of Meniere's disease, it is important to note that they are not a substitute for medical treatment. Always work closely with a healthcare provider to develop a comprehensive treatment plan that addresses your individual needs.

Diet and Nutrition for Meniere's

Diet and nutrition can play an important role in managing symptoms of Meniere's disease. Certain foods and beverages may trigger symptoms or exacerbate existing symptoms, while others may help to reduce symptoms. Here are some tips for a Meniere's-friendly diet:

Reduce sodium intake: High sodium intake can lead to fluid retention, which can exacerbate symptoms of Meniere's disease. It is recommended that individuals with Meniere's disease limit their sodium intake to less than 1,500 milligrams per day. This may involve avoiding processed foods, which are often high in sodium, and opting for fresh, whole foods instead.

Stay hydrated: Drinking enough water is important for overall health and may also help to reduce symptoms of Meniere's disease. Aim to drink at least eight cups of water per day, and consider drinking coconut water, which is high in electrolytes and may help to reduce fluid retention.

Avoid trigger foods: Certain foods may trigger symptoms of Meniere's disease in some people. Common trigger foods include caffeine, alcohol, chocolate, aged cheeses, and processed meats. Pay attention to your symptoms and try to identify any foods that may trigger them.

Eat anti-inflammatory foods: Inflammation can contribute to symptoms of Meniere's disease. Eating a diet that is rich in anti-inflammatory foods, such as leafy greens, berries, fatty fish, and nuts, may help to reduce inflammation and improve symptoms.

Consider supplements: Certain supplements may help to reduce symptoms of Meniere's disease. For example, magnesium supplements may help to reduce vertigo, while vitamin B6 supplements may help to reduce tinnitus. However, it is important to speak with a healthcare provider before taking any new supplements.

Eat regularly: Skipping meals or going too long without eating can lead to low blood sugar, which may exacerbate symptoms of Meniere's disease. Aim to eat regular meals and snacks throughout the day to maintain stable blood sugar levels.

Consider a low-carb or ketogenic diet: Some people with Meniere's disease have reported success with low-carb or ketogenic diets. These diets involve limiting carbohydrate intake and increasing fat intake, which can help to reduce inflammation and stabilize blood sugar levels.

Overall, a Meniere's-friendly diet involves eating fresh, whole foods, limiting sodium and trigger foods, and prioritizing anti-inflammatory foods. By making dietary changes and working closely with a healthcare provider, individuals with Meniere's disease may be able to reduce their symptoms and improve their quality of life.

Exercise and Physical Therapy

Exercise and physical therapy can be important components of managing Meniere's disease. Regular exercise can help to improve balance, reduce stress, and boost overall physical and mental health. Physical therapy can also be beneficial for individuals with Meniere's disease, as it can help to improve balance and reduce symptoms.

Here are some exercises and physical therapy techniques that may be helpful for individuals with Meniere's disease:

Balance exercises: Balance exercises can help to improve balance and reduce symptoms of dizziness and vertigo. Examples of balance exercises include standing on one foot, walking heel-to-toe, and performing yoga poses that challenge balance, such as tree pose or warrior III.

Tai chi: Tai chi is a gentle form of exercise that combines slow, flowing movements with deep breathing and meditation. Tai chi has been shown to be effective for improving balance and reducing symptoms of dizziness and vertigo in individuals with Meniere's disease.

Vestibular rehabilitation therapy: Vestibular rehabilitation therapy (VRT) is a type of physical therapy that focuses on improving balance and reducing symptoms of dizziness and vertigo. VRT may involve exercises such as eye movements, head movements, and balance training.

Cardiovascular exercise: Cardiovascular exercise, such as

walking, running, or swimming, can help to improve overall physical health and reduce stress. However, individuals with Meniere's disease should avoid activities that involve rapid head movements or jumping, as these can trigger symptoms.

Stretching: Stretching can help to improve flexibility and reduce muscle tension, which may contribute to symptoms of Meniere's disease. Stretching exercises may include neck stretches, shoulder stretches, and hamstring stretches.

Relaxation techniques: Stress can exacerbate symptoms of Meniere's disease, so practicing relaxation techniques such as deep breathing, meditation, or yoga may be helpful for reducing stress and improving overall wellbeing.

It is important for individuals with Meniere's disease to work closely with a healthcare provider to determine which exercises and physical therapy techniques are most appropriate for their specific needs and abilities. Some individuals may need to modify certain exercises or avoid certain activities altogether to avoid exacerbating symptoms.

Overall, regular exercise and physical therapy can be important components of managing Meniere's disease. By incorporating these strategies into their daily routines, individuals with Meniere's disease may be able to improve their balance, reduce symptoms, and improve their overall quality of life.

Managing Stress and Anxiety

Stress and anxiety can be significant triggers for symptoms of Meniere's disease. As such, learning how to manage stress and anxiety can be an important part of managing this condition. Here are some strategies that may be helpful for individuals with Meniere's disease:

Practice relaxation techniques: Deep breathing, meditation, and yoga are all effective techniques for reducing stress and anxiety. By incorporating these techniques into your daily routine, you may be able to reduce the frequency and severity of Meniere's symptoms.

Get enough sleep: Lack of sleep can exacerbate stress and anxiety, so it is important to make sure you are getting enough sleep each night. Aim for 7-8 hours of sleep each night and establish a consistent sleep schedule.

Exercise regularly: Regular exercise can help to reduce stress and anxiety, improve overall physical and mental health, and reduce symptoms of Meniere's disease. Try to get at least 30 minutes of moderate-intensity exercise most days of the week.

Avoid caffeine and alcohol: Caffeine and alcohol can both exacerbate symptoms of Meniere's disease and increase feelings of stress and anxiety. Try to limit your intake of these substances, or avoid them altogether.

Practice mindfulness: Mindfulness involves being present in the moment and fully engaged in your surroundings. By practicing mindfulness, you may be able to reduce feelings of stress and anxiety and improve your ability to cope with Meniere's symptoms.

Seek support: Talking to a therapist or joining a support group can be helpful for managing stress and anxiety related to Meniere's disease. These resources can provide a safe space to discuss your feelings and develop coping strategies.

Take breaks: It can be helpful to take breaks throughout the day to rest and recharge. Take a few deep breaths, go for a walk, or engage in another relaxing activity to help reduce stress and anxiety.

Identify triggers: It can be helpful to identify specific triggers for stress and anxiety related to Meniere's disease. Once you have identified these triggers, you can work on developing strategies to avoid or manage them.

It is important to remember that managing stress and anxiety is an ongoing process. What works for one person may not work for another, so it is important to experiment with different strategies and find what works best for you. By incorporating these strategies into your daily routine, you may be able to reduce stress and anxiety, improve your ability to cope with Meniere's symptoms, and improve your overall quality of life.

Coping with Hearing Loss

Hearing loss is a common symptom of Meniere's disease, and it can be challenging to cope with the changes it brings to your life. Here are some strategies that may be helpful for coping with hearing loss:

Use hearing aids: Hearing aids can help to amplify sounds and make them easier to hear. There are many different types of hearing aids available, so it is important to work with an audiologist to find the right one for you.

Seek support: Talking to friends and family about your hearing loss can help to reduce feelings of isolation and provide emotional support. Joining a support group for individuals with hearing loss can also be helpful.

Communicate effectively: When talking with others, make sure to speak clearly and ask them to do the same. Avoid talking in noisy environments or places with poor acoustics, and use visual cues like facial expressions and gestures to help you understand what others are saying.

Consider assistive listening devices: Assistive listening devices like FM systems and captioning can help to improve communication in challenging listening environments.

Practice good self-care: Taking care of your overall health can help to reduce the impact of hearing loss on your life. Exercise regularly, eat a healthy diet, and get enough sleep.

Balancing Work and Meniere's

Meniere's disease can present many challenges for individuals trying to maintain employment. Fluctuating symptoms, hearing loss, and balance issues can all impact job performance and career advancement. However, with proper planning and management, it is possible to balance work and Meniere's disease.

Communicate with your employer: It is important to communicate with your employer about your Meniere's disease and how it impacts your work. Discuss any necessary accommodations, such as flexible work hours, working from home, or reduced workload. The Americans with Disabilities Act (ADA) requires employers to provide reasonable accommodations for employees with disabilities, including those with Meniere's disease.

Plan for symptom management: Fluctuating symptoms can make it challenging to plan work activities. However, by keeping a symptom journal and tracking triggers, it is possible to identify patterns and plan accordingly. This may involve scheduling appointments or meetings for times of day when symptoms are less severe or taking regular breaks throughout the day to rest and manage symptoms.

Manage stress: Stress can exacerbate Meniere's disease symptoms, so it is important to develop effective stress management strategies. This may involve practicing relaxation techniques, such as meditation or deep breathing, or seeking support from a therapist or support group.

Use assistive technology: There are many assistive technologies available that can help individuals with Meniere's disease to better manage their symptoms. This may include hearing aids, captioning services, or assistive listening devices.

Take care of yourself: Taking care of your overall health is important for managing Meniere's disease symptoms and maintaining employment. This includes eating a healthy diet, exercising regularly, and getting enough sleep.

Consider job flexibility: For some individuals, a traditional 9-to-5 job may not be the best fit. Consider exploring options such as freelance work, part-time work, or self-employment that may offer more flexibility and autonomy.

Advocate for yourself: It can be challenging to navigate the workplace with Meniere's disease, but it is important to advocate for yourself and your needs. This may involve requesting accommodations, speaking up when your needs are not being met, and educating coworkers and supervisors about your condition.

While balancing work and Meniere's disease can be challenging, with proper management and planning, it is possible to maintain employment and achieve career goals. By communicating with your employer, managing symptoms, and prioritizing self-care, you can take control of your career and improve your overall quality of life.

Meniere's and Relationships

Meniere's disease can affect not only an individual's physical health but also their personal relationships. The unpredictable nature of symptoms, including vertigo attacks and hearing loss, can impact social activities and communication with loved ones. However, with open communication and understanding, it is possible to maintain healthy relationships while living with Meniere's disease.

Educate your partner: One of the most important steps in maintaining a healthy relationship while living with Meniere's disease is to educate your partner about the condition. This can include explaining the symptoms, treatment options, and potential impact on daily life. Knowledge and understanding can help to reduce anxiety and stress for both you and your partner.

Communicate openly: Effective communication is key to any relationship, but it is especially important when living with Meniere's disease. It is important to communicate openly about your symptoms, needs, and limitations. This can help your partner to better understand your experiences and to offer support and accommodations as needed.

Plan activities together: Meniere's disease symptoms can be unpredictable, but planning activities together can help to reduce anxiety and ensure that both partners are able to enjoy social events. This may involve planning activities that are less likely to trigger symptoms or that can be easily modified to accommodate your needs.

Seek support: Living with Meniere's disease can be challenging, but it is important to seek support from loved ones and professionals. This may include joining a support group, seeking therapy, or talking to a trusted friend or family member about your experiences.

Practice self-care: Taking care of your own physical and emotional health is important for maintaining healthy relationships. This may involve managing stress, practicing relaxation techniques, and prioritizing self-care activities that bring you joy and fulfillment.

Be patient: Living with Meniere's disease can be frustrating and challenging, but it is important to remember that your partner may also experience frustration and stress. It is important to be patient and understanding with each other, and to work together as a team to navigate the challenges of living with Meniere's disease.

Living with Meniere's disease can present many challenges, but with open communication, understanding, and support from loved ones, it is possible to maintain healthy relationships. By educating your partner, communicating openly, and practicing self-care, you can strengthen your relationships and improve your overall quality of life.

Meniere's and Mental Health

Living with Meniere's disease can be challenging, and the unpredictable nature of symptoms can take a toll on an individual's mental health. It is important for those living with Meniere's to prioritize their mental health and seek support when needed. In this chapter, we will explore the impact of Meniere's disease on mental health and offer strategies for coping with the emotional challenges of living with this condition.

Impact of Meniere's on Mental Health

Meniere's disease can have a significant impact on an individual's mental health. The unpredictability of symptoms, including vertigo attacks, hearing loss, and tinnitus, can lead to feelings of anxiety, depression, and frustration. The impact of Meniere's on mental health can be further compounded by the social isolation that may result from the need to limit activities and avoid triggers.

Coping with the Emotional Challenges of Meniere's

Seek support: It is important to seek support from loved ones, friends, and professionals. This may include joining a support group, talking to a therapist, or speaking with a trusted friend or family member about your experiences. Support can help you to feel less alone and provide you with coping strategies to manage your emotional challenges.

Practice relaxation techniques: Relaxation techniques, such as deep breathing, meditation, or yoga, can help to reduce anxiety and stress. Incorporating these techniques into your daily routine can help you to feel more grounded and centered.

Stay active: Engaging in regular physical activity can help to improve mood and reduce stress. Even low-impact activities, such as walking or swimming, can provide significant benefits.

Prioritize self-care: Prioritizing self-care activities, such as taking a bath, reading a book, or listening to music, can help you to feel more relaxed and rejuvenated. It is important to take time for yourself and prioritize activities that bring you joy and fulfillment.

Communicate with loved ones: Communicating openly with loved ones about your experiences can help to reduce feelings of isolation and anxiety. It is important to communicate your needs and limitations, and to work together to find solutions to challenges that arise.

Manage stress: Managing stress is an important aspect of coping with Meniere's disease. This may involve practicing stress management techniques, such as mindfulness, or making lifestyle changes to reduce stress levels.

Conclusion

Living with Meniere's disease can be challenging, and the impact on mental health should not be underestimated. It is important to prioritize mental health and seek support when needed. Coping strategies, such as seeking support, practicing relaxation techniques, and prioritizing self-care, can help to reduce feelings of anxiety and stress. With the right strategies in place, it is possible to maintain good mental health while living with Meniere's disease.

Finding Support and Resources

Living with Meniere's disease can be challenging, and finding support and resources can make a significant difference in managing the condition. In this chapter, we will explore the various resources available to individuals living with Meniere's disease and provide strategies for accessing the support you need.

Support Groups

Joining a Meniere's disease support group can provide a sense of community and support for individuals living with the condition. Support groups may be online or in-person and can offer a safe space to share experiences, ask questions, and receive emotional support. Many organizations, such as the Meniere's Society and the American Tinnitus Association, offer support groups and resources for individuals living with Meniere's disease.

Online Communities

In addition to support groups, online communities can be a valuable resource for individuals living with Meniere's disease. Online forums, social media groups, and online chat rooms can provide a platform for individuals to connect with others, share experiences, and ask questions. Online communities can also provide access to resources and information that may not be available locally.

Professional Support

In addition to support groups and online communities, professional support can also be helpful for individuals living with Meniere's disease. A primary care physician or an ENT specialist can provide medical advice and treatment options, while a therapist can offer emotional support and coping strategies. Occupational therapists can also provide strategies for managing daily activities and maintaining independence.

National Organizations

National organizations, such as the Meniere's Society and the American Tinnitus Association, provide resources and information for individuals living with Meniere's disease. These organizations offer educational materials, support groups, and online resources, and may also advocate for research and public policy initiatives related to Meniere's disease.

Assistive Technology

Assistive technology can also be a helpful resource for individuals living with Meniere's disease. Hearing aids can improve hearing loss, while cochlear implants may be an option for individuals with severe hearing loss. Sound therapy devices, such as white noise machines or hearing aids with sound masking capabilities, can also provide relief from tinnitus.

Local Resources

In addition to national resources, there may be local resources available to individuals living with Meniere's disease. This may include community support groups, rehabilitation services, or advocacy organizations. Local hospitals or medical centers may also offer Meniere's disease clinics or support groups.

Conclusion

Finding support and resources is an important aspect of managing Meniere's disease. Support groups, online communities, professional support, national organizations, assistive technology, and local resources are all valuable resources for individuals living with Meniere's disease. It is important to explore these resources and find the support you need to manage the challenges of living with Meniere's disease.

Protecting Your Hearing

Hearing loss is a common symptom of Meniere's disease, and it is essential to take steps to protect your hearing to prevent further damage. In this chapter, we will discuss strategies for protecting your hearing and reducing the risk of hearing loss.

Limiting Exposure to Loud Noise

Exposure to loud noise is a significant risk factor for hearing loss, and it is essential to limit exposure to loud noise to protect your hearing. This may include wearing earplugs or noise-cancelling headphones in loud environments, such as concerts or sporting events. It is also important to be mindful of noise levels in everyday activities, such as listening to music or using power tools.

Maintaining a Safe Distance from Loud Noise

In addition to limiting exposure to loud noise, it is also important to maintain a safe distance from loud noise sources. This may include sitting further away from speakers at concerts or using a lawn mower or leaf blower from a distance.

Taking Breaks from Noise

Taking breaks from noise is another important strategy for protecting your hearing. This may include taking a break from loud activities, such as listening to music or using power tools, or taking a break from noisy environments, such as restaurants or bars.

Using Hearing Protection

Hearing protection devices, such as earplugs or noise-cancelling headphones, can also be helpful in protecting your hearing. It is essential to choose hearing protection devices that are comfortable and effective in reducing noise levels. Custom-made earplugs or headphones may provide the best protection and comfort.

Monitoring Volume Levels

Monitoring volume levels is another important strategy for protecting your hearing. Many devices, such as smartphones and MP3 players, have volume limit settings that can help reduce the risk of hearing loss. It is important to be mindful of volume levels when using these devices and to take breaks to rest your ears.

Maintaining Overall Health

Maintaining overall health is also important in protecting your hearing. This includes getting regular exercise, eating a healthy diet, and managing stress levels. High blood pressure and other health conditions can also contribute to hearing loss, so it is important to manage these conditions as well.

Conclusion

Protecting your hearing is an important aspect of managing Meniere's disease. Limiting exposure to loud noise, maintaining a safe distance from loud noise sources, taking breaks from noise, using hearing protection, monitoring volume levels, and maintaining overall health are all important strategies for protecting your hearing. It is essential to be mindful of the risks of hearing loss and to take steps to protect your hearing to prevent further damage.

Sleep and Meniere's

Sleep is an essential part of our lives. It is important for physical, mental, and emotional well-being. However, people with Meniere's disease often find it difficult to get a good night's sleep due to the symptoms of the condition. The unpredictable and disruptive nature of the symptoms can make it challenging to fall asleep, stay asleep, and wake up feeling refreshed. In this chapter, we will explore the impact of Meniere's disease on sleep and strategies to improve sleep quality.

Impact of Meniere's on Sleep

Meniere's disease can affect sleep in several ways. The most common symptoms of Meniere's, such as vertigo, tinnitus, and hearing loss, can interfere with sleep. People with Meniere's often experience sudden and unpredictable vertigo attacks that can be accompanied by nausea, vomiting, and sweating. These symptoms can be frightening and disruptive, making it difficult to relax and fall asleep. Additionally, tinnitus, which is a ringing or buzzing sound in the ears, can be particularly bothersome at night when there are no other sounds to distract from it. Hearing loss can also impact sleep. People with hearing loss may be more sensitive to sounds and require a quieter environment to sleep. Additionally, they may need to use a hearing aid or other assistive devices to hear better, which can be uncomfortable or disruptive while sleeping.

Strategies to Improve Sleep Quality

There are several strategies that people with Meniere's disease can use to improve their sleep quality. The first step is to establish a consistent sleep routine. This means going to bed and waking up at the same time every day, even on weekends. It can also be helpful to establish a relaxing bedtime routine, such as taking a warm bath, reading a book, or listening to calming music. This routine signals to the body that it is time to sleep and can promote relaxation.

Creating a sleep-conducive environment is also important. This means keeping the bedroom cool, dark, and quiet. People with Meniere's may need to use earplugs or a white noise machine to block out external sounds. They may also need to use blackout curtains or an eye mask to block out light.

Managing symptoms of Meniere's disease is crucial for improving sleep quality. This may involve taking medication to control vertigo or tinnitus, using hearing aids or other assistive devices, or engaging in physical therapy to improve balance and reduce vertigo. Additionally, stress and anxiety can exacerbate Meniere's symptoms, so finding ways to manage stress, such as through mindfulness meditation or yoga, can also improve sleep quality.

It is also important to avoid stimulants that can disrupt sleep, such as caffeine, nicotine, and alcohol. These substances can interfere with the body's natural sleep-wake cycle and make it difficult to fall asleep or stay asleep.

Finally, if sleep disturbances persist despite these strategies, it may be helpful to consult a healthcare provider. They can evaluate for other sleep disorders, such as sleep apnea or insomnia, and provide additional treatment options.

Conclusion

Getting enough quality sleep is essential for overall health and well-being, especially for people with Meniere's disease who may experience disruptions due to the symptoms of the condition. By establishing a consistent sleep routine, creating a sleep-conducive environment, managing symptoms, and avoiding stimulants, people with Meniere's can improve their sleep quality. It is also important to seek medical advice if sleep disturbances persist, as there may be other underlying sleep disorders that require treatment. With the right strategies and support, people with Meniere's disease can improve their sleep quality and feel more rested and refreshed.

Preventing Triggers and Flare-Ups in Meniere's Disease

Meniere's disease is a chronic condition that can greatly impact a person's quality of life. The unpredictable nature of its symptoms can make it difficult to manage, but there are ways to prevent triggers and flare-ups that can help individuals with Meniere's to maintain some level of control over their condition. In this chapter, we will discuss some of the common triggers of Meniere's disease and provide tips for managing and preventing flare-ups.

Keep track of your symptoms

One of the best ways to prevent Meniere's flare-ups is to keep a record of your symptoms. This will allow you to identify any patterns or triggers that may be causing your symptoms to worsen. Make a note of when your symptoms occur, how long they last, and what activities you were engaged in at the time. This information can help you identify triggers and avoid them in the future.

Reduce stress

Stress can be a major trigger for Meniere's symptoms. Stress can cause a spike in cortisol, a hormone that can affect the inner ear and lead to vertigo, tinnitus, and hearing loss. To prevent flare-ups, it's important to manage stress through relaxation techniques such as deep breathing, meditation, or yoga.

Get enough sleep

Sleep is essential for overall health and well-being, and it can also play a role in managing Meniere's symptoms. Lack of sleep can lead to increased stress and anxiety, which can trigger symptoms. Aim to get at least 7-8 hours of sleep each night to reduce the risk of flare-ups.

Limit caffeine and alcohol

Caffeine and alcohol are both known triggers of Meniere's disease. They can affect the fluid levels in the inner ear and cause symptoms to worsen. Limiting or avoiding these substances can help to prevent flare-ups.

Avoid smoking

Smoking can also have a negative impact on Meniere's symptoms. Nicotine can cause blood vessels to constrict, which can affect blood flow to the inner ear and lead to vertigo and hearing loss. Quitting smoking or avoiding exposure to secondhand smoke can help to prevent flare-ups.

Maintain a healthy diet

A healthy diet can help to manage Meniere's symptoms by reducing inflammation in the body. Focus on consuming whole, nutrient-dense foods and limit processed foods and sugar. Incorporate foods that are high in antioxidants, such as berries and leafy greens, to reduce inflammation.

Stay hydrated

Dehydration can also trigger Meniere's symptoms, so it's important to stay hydrated by drinking plenty of water throughout the day. Avoid consuming beverages that can dehydrate the body, such as sugary drinks and alcohol.

Avoid rapid head movements

Rapid head movements can trigger vertigo in individuals with Meniere's disease. Avoid sudden head movements such as quick turns, bending over, or looking up.

Be aware of your environment

Certain environmental factors can trigger Meniere's symptoms, such as bright or flashing lights, loud noises, or strong odors. Be aware of your surroundings and avoid situations that may trigger symptoms.

Talk to your healthcare provider

If you're experiencing frequent or severe Meniere's symptoms, talk to your healthcare provider. They can work with you to develop a treatment plan that may include medication, physical therapy, or other interventions. Your provider may also recommend vestibular rehabilitation therapy, which can help to improve balance and reduce the frequency and severity of Meniere's symptoms.

Planning for Emergencies

Living with Meniere's disease can be challenging, especially when unexpected vertigo attacks occur. In some cases, these attacks can happen at the most inconvenient times, such as when driving or at work, and can cause safety concerns. That's why it's important to plan ahead and be prepared for emergencies related to Meniere's disease. Here are some tips to help you plan for emergencies and ensure your safety.

Develop an Emergency Plan

It's important to develop a plan for emergencies related to Meniere's disease, especially if you live alone. Talk to your doctor about creating a personalized plan that includes steps to take during a vertigo attack, such as lying down and keeping your eyes closed to reduce dizziness. You may also want to consider investing in a medical alert bracelet or necklace that provides information about your condition and emergency contact information.

Communicate with Your Loved Ones

Let your loved ones know about your condition and what to do in case of an emergency. Share your emergency plan with them, including instructions on how to get in touch with your doctor and other healthcare providers. It's also a good idea to keep a list of important phone numbers, such as your doctor's office, emergency contacts, and local hospitals, in an easily accessible place.

Plan for Transportation

If you experience vertigo attacks while driving, it's important to plan for transportation in case of an emergency. Consider having a trusted friend or family member on standby to pick you up if needed. You may also want to explore public transportation options in your area, such as buses or taxis.

Prepare an Emergency Kit

Prepare an emergency kit that includes essential items you may need during a vertigo attack, such as medication, water, snacks, and a comfortable pillow or cushion. Keep the kit in a place that's easily accessible, such as a bedside table or a designated emergency bag.

Inform Your Employer

If you have a job, it's important to inform your employer about your condition and any accommodations you may need in case of an emergency. Consider discussing options such as working remotely or adjusting your work schedule to avoid times when you're most likely to experience vertigo attacks.

Practice Self-Care

Taking care of yourself can help reduce the frequency and severity of vertigo attacks. Make sure to get enough rest, eat a healthy diet, and stay hydrated. Practice stress-reducing techniques such as meditation or deep breathing exercises, which can help you stay calm during a vertigo attack.

Stay Calm

Finally, it's important to stay calm during an emergency related to Meniere's disease. Remember that vertigo attacks typically only last a few minutes to a few hours and that you will feel better eventually. Stay positive and focused on your emergency plan, and seek medical attention if necessary.

In conclusion, planning for emergencies related to Meniere's disease can help ensure your safety and peace of mind. By developing an emergency plan, communicating with loved ones, planning for transportation, preparing an emergency kit, informing your employer, practicing self-care, and staying calm, you can be prepared for unexpected vertigo attacks and feel more in control of your condition. Remember to talk to your doctor about any concerns you may have and to seek medical attention if necessary.

Meniere's and Pregnancy

Meniere's disease can be a challenging condition to manage, and it can become even more complex during pregnancy. Although Meniere's does not pose a direct threat to pregnancy, it can still present unique challenges to women with the condition. In this chapter, we will explore how Meniere's disease can affect pregnancy and what women can do to manage the condition during this important time in their lives.

Meniere's Disease and Pregnancy: Understanding the Risks Pregnancy can trigger an increase in symptoms of Meniere's disease. Hormonal fluctuations that occur during pregnancy can cause changes in fluid levels in the inner ear, leading to increased vertigo and tinnitus. Additionally, changes in blood pressure and increased stress can also exacerbate Meniere's symptoms.

Although Meniere's disease does not pose a direct threat to pregnancy, some medications commonly used to treat the condition may not be safe during pregnancy. For example, diuretics like hydrochlorothiazide can reduce blood volume and lower blood pressure, which can be dangerous for both the mother and the fetus. Some antihistamines and sedatives can also cause drowsiness and affect the developing fetus.

Managing Meniere's Disease During Pregnancy

Managing Meniere's disease during pregnancy can be challenging, but there are several strategies that women can use to minimize symptoms and improve their overall quality of life.

Monitor Symptoms Closely: Pregnant women with Meniere's disease should be vigilant about monitoring their symptoms. This can help them identify triggers and take steps to minimize their impact.

Talk to a Doctor: It's important for pregnant women with Meniere's disease to consult with their doctor before starting or stopping any medications. Some drugs that are commonly used to treat Meniere's disease may not be safe during pregnancy.

Stay Hydrated: Drinking plenty of fluids can help maintain proper fluid balance in the body, which can reduce the severity of Meniere's symptoms.

Get Adequate Rest: Pregnancy can be exhausting, so it's important to get plenty of rest. Fatigue can exacerbate Meniere's symptoms, so it's important to prioritize rest and relaxation.

Avoid Triggers: Certain triggers, such as stress, caffeine, and alcohol, can exacerbate Meniere's symptoms. Pregnant women with Meniere's disease should be mindful of these triggers and avoid them whenever possible.

Consider Alternative Therapies: Many alternative therapies, such as acupuncture and yoga, can be effective in managing Meniere's symptoms. However, pregnant women should consult with their doctor before starting any new therapies.

Join a Support Group: Joining a support group can be an effective way for pregnant women with Meniere's disease to connect with others who are going through similar experiences. This can help provide emotional support and practical advice.

Conclusion

Pregnancy can be a challenging time for women with Meniere's disease, but it is still possible to manage the condition effectively. By monitoring symptoms, staying hydrated, getting adequate rest, and avoiding triggers, women can reduce the severity of Meniere's symptoms during pregnancy. Additionally, consulting with a doctor, considering alternative therapies, and joining a support group can also be effective strategies for managing the condition. With proper care and attention, women with Meniere's disease can enjoy a safe and healthy pregnancy.

Meniere's and Children

Meniere's disease is not limited to adults only, it can also affect children. Although it is not very common in children, it can cause significant problems in their lives. Meniere's disease can impact the development and growth of a child, as it can cause problems with balance, coordination, and hearing. In this chapter, we will discuss Meniere's disease in children, including its symptoms, causes, diagnosis, and treatment options.

Symptoms

The symptoms of Meniere's disease in children are similar to those in adults. The most common symptoms include:

Vertigo: This is a feeling of spinning or dizziness that can be quite severe and debilitating.

Tinnitus: This is a ringing, buzzing, or other noise in the ear that is not caused by an external sound.

Hearing loss: This can range from mild to severe and can affect one or both ears.

A feeling of fullness or pressure in the ear: This can be quite uncomfortable and can make it difficult to hear.

In children, Meniere's disease can also cause developmental delays, as the balance and coordination problems associated with the condition can affect their ability to learn and move around.

Causes

The exact cause of Meniere's disease in children is unknown, but it is believed to be related to a problem with the inner ear. This can include a buildup of fluid in the inner ear or a problem with the nerve that sends signals from the inner ear to the brain. Meniere's disease may also be related to genetics or a viral infection.

Diagnosis

Diagnosing Meniere's disease in children can be challenging, as the symptoms can be vague and difficult to describe. The doctor will typically conduct a physical exam, including a hearing test and balance test, to help diagnose the condition. They may also order imaging tests, such as an MRI or CT scan, to look for any abnormalities in the inner ear.

Treatment

Treatment for Meniere's disease in children will depend on the severity of the symptoms and the underlying cause of the condition. The goal of treatment is to manage symptoms and improve quality of life. Treatment options may include:

Medications: Medications, such as anti-nausea drugs and steroids, may be prescribed to manage symptoms.

Lifestyle changes: Changes to the child's diet or exercise routine may help manage symptoms.

Therapy: Physical therapy may be recommended to help improve balance and coordination.

Surgery: In severe cases, surgery may be necessary to remove excess fluid from the inner ear or repair any damage.

In addition to medical treatment, children with Meniere's disease may benefit from support from family, friends, and teachers. A supportive environment can help reduce stress and improve overall well-being.

Conclusion

Meniere's disease can affect children and can have a significant impact on their development and quality of life. Symptoms can include vertigo, tinnitus, hearing loss, and a feeling of fullness in the ear. Diagnosis can be challenging, but treatment options include medication, lifestyle changes, therapy, and surgery. With proper treatment and support, children with Meniere's disease can manage their symptoms and live a full and healthy life. It is important for parents and caregivers to be aware of the signs and symptoms of Meniere's disease and to seek medical attention if they suspect their child may be affected.

Navigating the Healthcare System

Navigating the healthcare system can be challenging for anyone, but it can be especially difficult for those with Meniere's disease. From finding the right healthcare provider to getting the proper treatment, it can be overwhelming. However, understanding the healthcare system and knowing your rights as a patient can help you receive the best care possible.

Finding the Right Healthcare Provider

The first step in navigating the healthcare system is to find the right healthcare provider. This can be a primary care physician, an otolaryngologist (ear, nose, and throat specialist), or a neurologist. When choosing a healthcare provider, it is important to consider their experience and expertise in treating Meniere's disease.

It is also important to consider the location and accessibility of the healthcare provider's office. Meniere's disease can cause vertigo, making it difficult to travel long distances or navigate public transportation. Choosing a healthcare provider who is close to your home or work can make it easier to attend appointments.

Getting a Diagnosis

Getting a proper diagnosis for Meniere's disease can also be challenging. The symptoms of Meniere's disease can be similar to other conditions, such as migraines or inner ear infections. However, Meniere's disease has specific diagnostic criteria that healthcare providers use to make a diagnosis.

If you suspect you have Meniere's disease, it is important to discuss your symptoms with your healthcare provider. They may refer you to an otolaryngologist or neurologist for further evaluation and testing. This may include hearing tests, balance tests, and imaging tests, such as an MRI.

Insurance Coverage

Navigating insurance coverage can also be a challenge when seeking treatment for Meniere's disease. Some insurance plans may not cover certain treatments or procedures, such as vestibular rehabilitation therapy or surgery. It is important to understand your insurance coverage and discuss any potential out-of-pocket costs with your healthcare provider.

Additionally, if you have a disability due to Meniere's disease, you may be eligible for Social Security Disability Insurance (SSDI) or Supplemental Security Income (SSI). These programs can help provide financial assistance if you are unable to work due to your condition.

Advocating for Yourself

As a patient, it is important to advocate for yourself and your health. This includes asking questions, seeking second opinions, and discussing your treatment options with your healthcare provider. You have the right to be an active participant in your healthcare decisions.

It can also be helpful to keep a record of your symptoms, treatment, and medications. This can provide important information for your healthcare provider and help track your progress.

Support Groups and Resources

Support groups and resources can also be helpful in navigating the healthcare system. These resources can provide information and support for individuals with Meniere's disease and their families. The Meniere's Disease Foundation and the American Tinnitus Association are two organizations that provide support and resources for individuals with Meniere's disease.

In conclusion, navigating the healthcare system can be challenging for individuals with Meniere's disease. However, finding the right healthcare provider, understanding insurance coverage, advocating for yourself, and accessing support groups and resources can help you receive the best care possible. By being an active participant in your healthcare decisions, you can take control of your health and manage your Meniere's disease effectively.

Endnote

Meniere's disease can be a challenging condition to manage, but with the right knowledge and support, it is possible to live a fulfilling life. This self-help book has provided an in-depth look at Meniere's disease, including its symptoms, causes, treatment options, and strategies for coping with its various challenges.

Throughout this book, we have emphasized the importance of taking a holistic approach to managing Meniere's disease. This includes not only addressing physical symptoms, but also considering mental health, lifestyle habits, and social support systems.

By implementing the strategies outlined in this book, including medication management, natural remedies, diet and exercise, stress reduction techniques, and hearing protection, those living with Meniere's disease can better manage their symptoms and improve their overall quality of life.

It is important to note that Meniere's disease is a complex condition, and what works for one person may not work for another. Therefore, it is crucial to work closely with healthcare professionals and seek out additional resources and support as needed.

Remember, you are not alone in your journey with Meniere's disease. There are many resources and support systems available, including advocacy organizations, support groups, and healthcare professionals who specialize in treating this condition. With determination, resilience, and the right tools, it is possible to navigate the challenges of Meniere's disease and live a full and fulfilling life.